90 *miles*

Pitt Poetry Series

Ed Ochester, Editor

90 *miles*

S E L E C T E D   A N D   N E W   P O E M S

Virgil Suárez

University of Pittsburgh Press

The publication of this book is supported by a grant
from the Pennsylvania Council on the Arts

PENNSYLVANIA
COUNCIL
ON THE
ARTS

Published by the University of Pittsburgh Press, Pittsburgh, PA 15260
Manufactured in the United States of America
Printed on acid-free paper
10 9 8 7 6 5 4 3 2 1
ISBN 0-8229-5880-5

for my wife & daughters,

who bridge the distances

Contents

New Poems

90 *miles*

The distance between Cuba and the United States
according to a mile marker at the southernmost
point in Key West, Florida, and where thousands
of Cubans have lost their lives and continue
to do so in their desperate journey to freedom.

from *You Come Singing*

Rice Comes to *El Volcán*

the corner *bodega* run by El Chino Chan
where when the food rations arrived

the people in Arroyo Naranjo, Cuba,
lined up and waited and listened as Chan

called out *"aló, aló,"* Spanish-Chinese
for *arroz*. Rice. I, six or seven, stood

in line with my mother in the shade
of the *guayaba* trees, watched as people

moved in and out of the sun and heat.
Women fanned their faces. Talk & gossip

buzzed like the horseflies that flew up
from the fields and brook. Chan told

stories of when the great Poet jumped
into the river and the villagers, to keep

the fish from eating the poet, tossed in
rice dumplings wrapped in bamboo leaves.

Rice. The blessing at weddings. Constant
staple with its richness of spirit. Sustenance.

Slowly the rations are filled and the line
moves and my mother and I reach the counter.

Behind it hang *papalotes,* kites made
of colorful rice paper, next to them

the countless oriental prints of carp,
dragons, tigers, and egrets. Chan talks

about the grain of rice kept in the glass
case at El Capitolio in the city, a love poem

written on it in print so small one needs
more than a magnifying glass to read

what it says. Chan, rice, magic—the gift
of something different to pass the time.

Now, so many miles and years from this life,
in the new place called home, rice,

like potatoes, goes unnoticed when served.
Often, my daughters ignore it and I won't

permit it. Rice, I say to them, needs respect,
their full attention, for blessed is that which

                    carries so many so far.

The Nuns in the Family

Here's my disclaimer: I don't know the first
thing about religion and I'm not religious.

My mother doesn't know this about me,
she likes to believe I still believe, still prays

to Saint Jude for my well-being. Whenever
the subject of religion comes up, I excuse

myself and go to the bathroom or pick up
a magazine. See, I don't want to come out

and blame the two nuns in our family, who
visited us in Madrid when we lived there

(thanks to them, my mother says, we were
able to get out of Cuba), but the two weeks

they spent with us, they took me to church
with them twice a day, once in the morning

and once in the late afternoon, at a time
when the children (eleven, like me) were out

playing soccer in the park, and there I was
with these two perfect strangers, dressed

like *hurracas,* walking to church. Two
weeks, and each visit they made me confess.

I confessed dry, made-up stuff when I ran
out of the usual mischief I told the screen

in the confessional. The voice behind
the screen always said the same thing, pray,

pray for your sins. What sins? I thought.
Each time during mass, I felt awkward—

when people stood, I sat, when they knelt,
I stood. What travesty. Then one day,

glorious with sunshine, as we walked to church,
a truck full of bulls headed for the plaza

stopped and a bull jumped out of the back
and ran down the street, headed directly

toward us, and when the nuns started to pray,
a man pushed me out of the way into a shop.

The bull kept running toward us until a *guardia
civil* took out his gun and shot the bull

right in front of the nuns. The bull's legs
buckled under and the animal fell at their feet.

The nuns crossed themselves, grabbed my hand,
and rushed me down the sidewalk toward church.

I told the story in the confessional, and there was
more silence than usual coming from behind

the screen. A miracle, said the voice finally.
Miracle? What miracle? I was confused,

and I said so, for which I was told to pray
more than ever before, in punishment.

The nuns never brought up the bull incident,
and after two weeks they left us for their convent

in Seville. So, these days when the nuns
in the family come up in conversation,

I start thinking about confessing stuff
I haven't even done, pure mischief,

like when I took off my big red T-shirt,
tapped on the door of the confessional,

and when the priest came out and put his fingers
up to his forehead to simulate the horns on a big

bad bull, I put the moves of the *matador* on him,
shouting (and you could hear the echoes

inside the basilica): ¡*Olé toro, olé toro,* HA!

Clotheslines

The day my mother stood in the kitchen
& cooked all the turtle meat from the turtles

I helped my father kill & she screamed
when the sizzling chunks started to jump

& we rushed in to check on what was up
& my father told her that it was okay,

that turtle meat always did that when fried
& then we got back to the slaughter of the pig

my father had bartered a dozen rabbits for
& when we finally cornered it at the end

of the walkway by the side of the house,
next to the chicken coop, it squealed & set

all the chickens aflutter & a cloud of dust
rose in the air, a combination of dirt & dung

& my father got something in his eyes
& he laughed & I sneezed & sneezed

& when the chickens settled down the pig
snuck by us & ran back to the patio

knocking on its way the stick holding up
my mother's clothesline & all the laundry

drying fell on the dirt & the pig trampled
it & it made my father so angry he took

the wire from the clothesline, looped it over
the pig's neck & when the pig stood still

my father reeled it in & with a broom handle
he applied a tourniquet to the pig

& with a final squeal it dropped on its front
knees, choked by the wire that cut so deep

blood spurted out onto everything, mainly
my mother's washed clothes & the pig stood

still long enough for my father to plunge
a knife into its heart. There we stood, my

father & I, out of breath, he with bloodied
arms & myself with the pangs of excitement

aflutter in my chest. Amazed by the slaughter
of so many animals in one afternoon, I stood

there quiet, caught in the splendor of my mother's
whitest laundry. My father put the clothesline

back up & one by one I picked up all
the garments from the ground & carried them

to my mother. My father leaned against
the door frame with a satisfied look on his face,

a smile on his lips. This was in Havana in 1968
& I have never seen my father more content.

Now when I travel on the open roads of the U.S.,
I look out across the expanse of peoples' yards

& when I see the clotheslines, heavy with laundry,
swaying in the breeze, & the fact someone

worked so hard at putting it up & out, I think
about how much debris, time, & distance

have kicked up into my eyes,

Luis Navarro Rubio Comes Singing

Caught between contemplation & smoke,
the pungent aroma of your Cohiba, the clink-
clank of family forever constant in the kitchen,
           you come singing.   *canta y repica*

A medley of Barbarito Diez songs: "*La mujer
de Antonio camina así, cuando va a el mercado,
camina así . . .*"
           you come singing.   *clave*

Between the endless noise & clutter of this in-
between, can't-do world, this shit-everywhere,
shit-all-the-time United States of *Los Americanos,*
           you come singing.   *guayo*

Just to kill time, you sit on the porch of the house
on Evergreen, South Gate, California, and think
about the past,
           you come singing.   *tambor*

Past the cane fields, *bohíos,* the oxen carts
on the way to the mill, leaving tracks
on the red dirt of your homeland,
           you come singing.   *tumba/baja*

Bola de Nieve's
"*Ay mamá, Ines, Ay mamá, Ines,
todos los negros tomamos café,*"
           you come singing.   *güiro*

The miniature roses help you pass the time
in this foreign land, away from the sugarcane,

sweet coffee, fields of tobacco,
        you come singing.   *tumba/alta*

Benny More: *"Maracaibo, este son pa'*
que tu lo bailes. En la Habana y en el campo,
todos lo quierén bailar!"
        You come singing.   *quijada*

Singing from Santiago de Cuba, Dominican
Republic, Los Angeles on Pico, then later
Plaska Avenue, singing.
        You come singing.   *pailas*

The aroma of roasted pork, fried *yuca,*
mojito criollo, all over the places
where you've been,
        you come singing.   *chékere*

You sit there & smoke & curse,
blaspheme that power that brought
you this far, so far away from *las palmas,*
        you come singing.   *trompeta*

The crystalline water and sand that glittered
with diamond dust—when you close your eyes,
the images wash over you & overwhelm you,
        you come singing.   *bongós*

You sit there and sing:
"Cachita esta alborota, ahora canta
el cha-cha-cha."
        You come singing.   *flauta*

The reality of this fate, this doom
thirty-six years in the making, springs

forth in the taste of bitter, watery coffee,
           you come singing.   *conga*

The stale whiteness of the daily bread,
the snarl of this wicked tongue
you'll never understand—too harsh,
           you come singing.   *contrabajo*

In the kitchen you sit there on your
favorite chair & listen to the white noise
emerging from the deep recesses,
           you come singing.   *cencerro*

Trio Matamoros: "*Mamá yo quiero saber
de donde son los cantantes, que los encuentro
muy galantes y los quiero conocer,*"
           you come singing.   *maraca*

Far from the island of the tobacco & the *son,*
your sweet land, of tobacco & *ron,*
pretty women—no land like it,
           you come singing.   *botija*

Past the Thrifty's on Slauson & Gage,
past the Pussycat Theater, past the tumult,
through the air, now, Luis, through red dirt,
           you go singing.   *timbales*

Past azure skies, telephone polls, & all
the goddamned technology of the ages,
past the pharmacies, *boticas,* and *bodegas,*
           you go singing.   *saxofóno*

To where the *tomeguín* & *azulejo*
nest in the low bushes, emerald jungle

of your youth, you go *cantando,*
           you go singing.   *clarinete*

The burn of your song is a scar
through the heart of this bicultural/bilingual
ambiguity & nightmare,
           you go singing.   *trompeta china*

You come & go singing, through the smoke
& clarity on your way home now. You are
on your way home, you choose home now,
           you go singing.   *bongó*

Luis Navarro Rubio, at rest in peace,
flesh & bone, listen now, father, son,
& ghost, as the wind rustles,
           you go singing.   *chancletas*

High atop the *palmeras,* your song echoes,
you arrive home now, like the mockingbird,
your song calls out & all the time
           you go singing.   *guitarra*

Your song calls out through the distance
of space & time for the rest of us,
for the rest of us to hurry home now,
           you go singing.   *canta y replica*

White Wall

I've decided the only thing that really interests me is how
the sun hits a white wall.

Edward Hopper to Andrew Wyeth

Somehow the crow snuck in, its caws echo
      in the fluorescence of the hallways.

We are all waiting at the ICU ward
      for your suffering to come to an end.

Tonight the full moon casts long shadows
      against the hospital wall. Lung cancer

has spread fast; the X-rays show
      the luminous bunches of grapes inside

your lungs. Within an hour of ruckus—
      between beeps, tics, bleeps—all those

white noises only discernible to the sick,
      the heart races to be nourished, first

by articles & prepositions (tell a little
      lie, call it a *Cuba Libre,*) next feeds

on the adverbs & adjectives, no
      need now for conjunctions. Leave

the verbs for last, that final option
      as the morphine works its magic,

pain held at bay for now. Out beyond
      the buoys, beyond where the opaline

turns to emerald green, an island
emerges, the island of your birth.

Listen, now, a conure cries out.
Your soul wants to make a quiet

entrance and take its place among
the *ceibas, framboyán,* and *palmeras,*

between the diamond dust sand
and the luscious foliage. The wind

announces your presence. Rest now;
rest finally. A rain falls and washes

memory away to become a new seed,
a sprout, a jungle, a man born infant.

But we return to this business
of white walls, the crow cassocked

in its vestibule of bleakness, blinded
by the hocus-pocus of the end

of the millennium. Inside penumbra,
the ebb of weak light confronts

the shadows upon the once white wall.
Your heart pulse rattles in your ears:

"Tienes dolor, Papi," a nurse wants
to know. Inside the morphine drip,

the sound of waves beckons you back,
then the sound of something hitting

an oxygen tank becomes the pealing
        of bells. Who stand privy to the mystery

of the concave? The women angels
        come to grip your hands that remain

bound up so you won't tug the tubes
        of the respirator. Next door they ready

a man for his third and possibly final
        surgery; his gut busted and the infection

is killing him. Who returns from such
        journeys? Your glazed eyes look

beyond the ceiling at the black buzzards
        (crows?) circling the sky. The veins

under the thin skin of your temples knot;
        you speak by knitting your brows,

batting your eyelids, you speak loudest
        with the bleeping of your heart monitor.

No words left to describe all the qualities
        of a white wall. Thus arrives the hour

of great stillness when the distant coastal
        lights flicker down to a slow beat

on the water's surface. The heart
        shimmers; its beat finds solace in the way

the moon casts long shadows against a white wall.

The Valet's Lament

E' la solita storia del pastore . . .
Il povero ragazzo
voleva raccontarla, e s'addormì
C'è nel sonno l'oblio.
Come l'invidio!

Francesco Cilea

The President's personal valet, a sort of Sancho
    Panza, retired in Hialeah, his life played out now.

Fishing. Dominoes with friends. Family visits
    on the weekends; only the few know he wept

for the third time in his life during the televised
    funerals, first the First Lady's, then his boss's.

Los Americanos, what a bunch of crazies.
    Every time he thinks he understands them, they

confuse him further. None of this sad history
    would have happened in Cuba, no sir. They took

a great man—they took him and worked him into
    weakness. During those years his job entailed

looking out for the President's well-being, providing
    sustenance. All those late-night club sandwiches,

the way he liked them without cheese. In those
    early morning hours, they sat in silence, in darkness,

among the tiles and white counters—they don't call
    it the White House for the lack of physical purity,

right? They sat in silence, and he watched as his boss
        ate. What bothered the President most was the name

thing: the liberties with the *X* as they took it and turned
        it into the swastika. The night they visited Lincoln

and all the students set upon them, he could tell
        nothing would ever be the same, not only in the house,

but with the man—he succumbed to all the pressures.
        They took a great man and broke him. That never

happened in Cuba. That was the joke they shared,
        when the President would smile and say: but it does,

Manolo, it does, it happens to great men everywhere.
        America's long night begun with Kennedy ended

with Nixon. The FBI people came and threatened
        he'd lose his job if he indulged the President's whim

ever again. No more such luxuries, the broken
        choices of a broken man. His job! What did it matter—

it would soon be all over for everyone in America.
        The fucking past, the fucking people, fucking

Democracy, *Democrazy,* none of it would happen
        in the old country, where power corrupted absolutely.

So they took a great man and made less of him. Broken,
        distraught, Manolo wept for the first time when his boss

addressed the White House staff, then later as he saluted
        from the helicopter. Manolo never wept again until

the televised funerals with Reverend Billy Graham,
the Girls and their families now. How sad, all of it.

Now he fishes, plays dominoes with friends at the park.
They all know his story, but nobody brings it up,

until those moments when Manolo's eyes well up
for no apparent reason, and then they ask what,

what is the matter with him, and he says nothing.
"None of it would have ever happened in Cuba."

The men nod in understanding. Manolo's lament,
the one he'd like to relate if he ever writes the book,

Views of a Great Man Broken, was that he failed
to reach over and hug the President when he most

needed to be hugged. But he didn't do it; he held
back, and now it has become his deepest regret

in all of American History. In America, the business
at hand is how to take great men and break them,

break them in like all those horses in the John Wayne
westerns, broken-in horses, but not this horse, no.

Heavy Metal Speaks

the centrifugal force that brings
                              us to Leon Iron & Scrap Metal
          on this bright but chilly November noon
                    heeds the call when the power
of words fails us, our lament, when art
                              surrenders to action. we must act
          charged by the instinct & yearn
                              for that which unravels & uncoils
                    the self. in the mood to salvage,
          we come in search of circles
                              & signs, something to make sense
          out of the heap of refuse. *cada loco*
con su tema. we consider the clutter
                    of waste, the dull silence of rust,
                the blind mesh of wire-like despair.
          avoid despair at all costs—that's the goal
                    of our hands. avoid *that* precipice—
                    for we know that precipice all too well
                & often the search's all we can do
        to survive the peril of our hands too close
        to the guns.   juiced-up firepower,
                              you explain the process in: *Passages*
        from the Middle: Basquiat's Door.
the horror of the trips
                              so far taken, about to, when the power
doesn't let go. it claims more lives
          everyday, but not ours. we won't get fooled
                    by charmless chain gods,
                          whose implements & tools of torture
                don't change through the centuries.
          shackles remain shackles. haven't they torn
                              enough tongues with the bit,

poked enough holes into the flesh, scarred,
                              cut, lacerated, mutilated, & bled
                    to get filled & sickened. what more does it want?
            what it demands now—what it refuses
                              to witness in the mirror of time & history—
                    it won't get from us.
        you work the blowtorch, hammer,
& scrape brush—weapons to break the circle
                              over the water, like the Eucharist
                    in the clean hands of a priest. you got *The Piano
            Lesson,* after Bearden, after Wilson.
                    your *Blues for J x 2,* Judas & Jesus
& the possibility of both being the same
                    man. the circle's broken, brother,
        but we stay afloat, circumnavigating
            the work of the mind & spirit fused with the labor
                of the hands. this is greater than any power.
        besides, even when the art fails us, which it won't,
                    there's still solace in the weight of the rock,
            the swiftness of the stick, of the idea that without us,
        the power loses, becomes power*less.*
the distance carries the sounds of your work
                              as you bend, mold,
                    & shape this metal, this heavy yet malleable
            metal. there's nothing it can do now but give under
                    the coax of your beautiful, wise spirit.
you figure that what has stirred in us
                cannot be broken, what we haven't given
                    cannot be taken, on this splendid day
        when we come to listen & heed
        what sorrows, what joys
                    of what the metal chooses to speak.

                                        In memory of Ed Love

from *Garabato Poems*

Lazarito & the Habanero Chilis

He was not all there, meaning he had been born
"with problems." That's what our parents said.

All his father ever said was "No Lazaro, No
Lazaro, No Lazaro!" But Lazaro was always

getting himself into trouble. He liked to run
naked out to the streets, then he would aim

his peepee at cars and urinate in big arcs.
His father would come running after him,

screaming, "Lazaro, Lazaro, *me vas a volver loco!*"
Then there was the time Lazaro snapped all the

habanero chilis off the plants that grew in his father's
garden, and he stuffed them in his mouth. Ah, the screams.

His parents had to call the ambulance, and when none
arrived, they asked Talo, our next-door neighbor

for a ride to the hospital. After the chili incident
we never heard from or saw Lazaro again, and his

parents came and went out of the house
as if they had been childless and content all their lives.

The Dirt Eaters

Whenever we grew tired and bored of curb ball,
    of encircling the scorpions we found under rocks

by the mother-in-law tongues within a fiery circle
    of kerosene and watching as they stung themselves

to death, we ate dirt: soft, grainy, pretend chocolate
    dirt, in our fantasies sent to us by distant relatives

in *El Norte. Fango.* We stood in a circle, wet the dirt
    under our bare feet, worked with our fingers to crumble

the clogs with our nails, removed the undesired twigs,
    pebbles, and beetles. Dirt—how delicious. How filling.

We ate our share of it back then. Beto, the youngest,
    warned us not to eat too much; it could make us sick,

vomit, give us the shits, or even worse, worms.
    We laughed. We ridiculed him. We chanted

after him: "*¡Lo que no mata, engorda!*
    ¡Lo que no mata, engorda!"

What doesn't kill you makes you fat, and stronger.

The Hatchery

Once in Havana as schoolchildren we took a field trip
to a chicken hatchery not too far from the school.

We walked there single file, already a string of blemished
pearls strung by our sweaty hands, divided every

tenth by a teacher. We wore our Young Pioneer uniforms,
and the sweat made our shirts stick to our backs, the half-

moons wet under our armpits. We walked through chambers
in the hatchery in awe of so much stainless steel, tiled

walls and granite floors, aluminum doors, walked silent
under the flicker of bad fluorescent lights. We got the tour:

eggs on the conveyor belts about to be cleaned of shit,
the sexing tables on which light passed through the eggs,

the incubator room with all the trays from the hatching room.
We walked through single file, passed rooms filled with the chirp

of thousands of baby chicks, a floor gone furry with the downy
white-yellow of baby chicks. The worker/guide explained

the process from fertile eggs to birth. In another room,
a collection of jars with all of nature's anomalies,

"left turns," as the man called these little accidents.
The specimens floated in formaldehyde, aliens from other worlds,

we said. The males, it was explained to us, the few born,
are gathered and separated and fed for only a few days,

then they are sent next door to the grinders. The world went
white and still when the guide said "*moledoras.*" The teachers

looked at the guide, eyes wide open, a sigh on their lips,
as if to stop him from going on about this horrible fate

of male chicks in the world of poultry. What happens there?
The male chicks are ground up and mixed with by-products

to make pellets for farm animals. We shivered at the news.
Later, we each received a chick to take home, a science project

of our own. Responsibility tests. We thought of the possibilities,
if the chicks we carried close would grow

to be roosters, or grow at all. No matter, for if they did grow,
they undoubtedly would end up in the soup. So many of us walked

home that afternoon with our prizes, some of us giddy with the idea
of feeding and nurturing. Our parents, the dissidents, who

wanted no part of the Revolution, would know what to do with such
a precious gift. We held our chicks close to our hearts,

and this memory of our visit to the hatchery in Havana lingers,
the yellow puffs scattered on the floor like dandelions, free

to float in the air at last, free to float away in the faint breeze
of memory, across the barren and ravaged fields we now

call our childhoods.

The Night Train Called *El Lechero*

My father rode it all over Cuba when he went foraging
for the food we needed back in the city, food to survive.

He went on long trips and always returned with fruit,
vegetables, the tubers like *yuca* and *boniato* my mother

fried up crispy in the lard of the pigs we slaughtered.
He brought back turtles, fish, venison meat, duck, chickens.

El Lechero, the milk train, traveled the island at night,
when the fireflies could easily be mistaken for stars.

Most of all, my father brought back stories, stories he told
to my mother and me, during the blackouts in Havana.

People on the move, like him looking, foraging for better
chances for themselves. Soldiers, prisoners on their way

to cut sugarcane, lovers coming to the city to get married.
My father told us the story of a man, like him, out to find

something to bring back to his family, a sack of rice he bartered
a pair of rabbits for, and the night rain soaked through the *yute*

sack, which unbeknownst to the man, had rotted, and when
the man lifted the sack it split down the center, and the rice

spilled down the steps of the crowded train where he and my
father had sat and talked of better days in their youth,

my father's breath almost blowing out the candles my mother
always put on the table, in case of a blackout, and the shine

in my father's eyes as he spoke of that man, like him, on his knees,
scooping up the rice with cupped hands, begging the rain

not to wash the rice that would nourish his family back home,
not to wash away like everything else in his life: home, family,

opportunity . . . and my father helps the man gather what little
rice is left, then both men sit there in the silence, dulled

by the rocking train, *El Lechero,* which still travels through
the island, where boys stay awake to listen for its whistle,

the clank-clank of its wheels, and in the silence it leaves
behind, the sound of men as they plead, plead with the night's

rain not to wash so much of their future away.

Mazorra, or House for the Incorrigible

Before the days of shock treatment
and needles, *pildoras* and juice,

this place in Havana, banana plants
outside its windows, housed

the infirmed of spirit, the politically
incorrect. Everyone abandoned

here in this place, the house
of the incorrigible, lost more

than track of time. Outside
the windows, the frogs beckoned

and sang their nuptial susurrus.
This house of crazy longing

became the place of puzzles,
endless glasses filled with pink

liquid—the frogs leapt and stuck
to the glass panes of the windows,

silhouetted by the moon. They ate
the insects dumb enough to succumb

to the light reflected there. Never
seek the source of light, you will never

find it here at Mazorra. Never ask
for the time. After the Revolution

so many fathers lost their way here.
One day gone from the neighborhood,

the next singing with the frogs. Avoid
the temptation to confess too much.

Our mothers threatened us
with the knowledge of this place, hid

in the deep woods, off the road,
on the outskirts of Havana,

with its luring gardens, its ponds,
its frogs and birds—its perishing

insects. This place so many childhood
friends came to know well in time,

or learned to forget about the time
in Mazorra after the Revolution.

The Seamstress

When she thinks of what is the one constant
        in her life, she thinks of the stitch. The way
the needle punctures cloth and sets

the thread. She remembers when she saw
        the Singer machine at her grandmother's
house, the woman with the cloudy eyes,

the black-gap mouth, the woman who
        told stories of witches by the bridge,
of specters by the side of country roads

who suckled on the blood of humans, of serpents
        who swallowed sugarcane cutters—asleep
under the shade of *framboyanes* and *mameyes*—whole,

the woman whose face appears in the wrinkles
        of the fabric she now sews together. She
loves the hum and vibrations of the machine's

motor, makes stitching a constant clatter
        much like the sound of the women of her childhood
who beat and cleaned rice in the hot morning

sun. She is alone now, the mother of a child
        grown and gone from her home, married with
children of his own. She is here in Hialeah,

alone in the three bedroom apartment her late
        husband, three months in the grave, worked
alongside her so hard for. They came to Los

Angeles in 1974, and from that beginning
         the constant she depended on was the sound
of an overlap machine stitching zippers to denim

pants, piecemeal, piecemeal—the pay never
         going higher than ten cents per piece. What comfort
is the sound of this machine her husband bought

for her. He knew what sewing means to her,
         the kind of disappearance she relished in her
childhood. Here she is, a widow, far from her

country of birth, far from her sisters and brothers.
         Her father still alive, her mother in the ground,
and quite suddenly she feels the urge to laugh,

laugh at how time weaves itself into the intricacies
         of the spirit, of the heart—she is planning a return
to the island of her birth, but first she will finish

this dress for her oldest granddaughter, a child
         born in this country, speaking no other language
than the language of her birthplace. What joy

she feels as the lace moves under her fingers,
         the dress almost finished, she will wear it, become
the child in the photos, travel back to her country,

go through the empty rooms of an empty house,
         feel the heat of her birthplace, hear the cries
of a child about to be born in 1938, San Pablo, Cuba.

On the Assembly Line

Cousin Irene worked in the cold of a warehouse
basement in New Jersey, soldering the filaments
to GE lightbulbs. The job required steady hands,
without gloves, bare fingers for sensitivity,
and her hands cramped up eventually, after six
hours or so, but the workday lasted ten or twelve,
in so much cold. This was her life for several
years in America—back home, in Cuba, she'd been
a chicken sexer, a botanist caring for orchids,
a potato peeler, a cigar ring paster, a picker
of papayas—all as a volunteer worker because she
wanted to leave the country. So in Trenton,
Union City, Elizabeth, at least she got paid
for the work she did with her hands, though her
choices continued to be blue-collar work, and she
thanked god for her hands, her reliable hands,
so necessary. She came to the United States
through the Peter Pan Project as a teenager
with the promise of a scholarship to an all-girl
boarding school in Kentucky, which never
materialized—she got as far as New Jersey.
Here, at night, she came home from the factory
and soaked her hands in warm soapy water.
She looked on as her fingers moved, these tendrils
of her once young hands—blessed these ten digits
that rooted her life to so much work and possibility.

Song for the Royal Palms of Miami

Everywhere they stand, slightly bent
against nocturnal offshore breezes,

as if strained to hear the susurrus of wind:
free, free, *libre*. . . . Dear Gustavo, when

we spoke of this catatonia befallen
our fathers, this inertia of mind and spirit,

we might have second-guessed their wills,
the dregs-like residue of hope left inside them; us.

Memories against the *"ventolera,"*
as my old man calls the winds of change.

Here he is at Palm Springs Hospital
recovering once again from major surgery,

this time the offensive being against colon
cancer. (Little do I know he will not,

not make it out.) Listen, we too struggle
against the uncertainty, pulled by the roots,

remembrance of our lost childhoods.

I think of you on this clear
November day, when outside the hospital

window, wind tussles the fronds
of a palm tree, not any palm tree, but a royal

palm tree, like the ones all over that island.
My father knows its name: *palmera.*

So does yours. They know the *palmiche,*
fed to pigs to fatten them up, the leaves

of the fronds used to make good hats;
the soft-pulp trunks can be dug
out to make canoes.

        They are everywhere,
these slender giants, proud, resolute

against the ravages of weather and time.
I say they are built to survive everything.

I say today they are mile markers of our
fathers' trip through exile, monuments

to their bravura of spirit—they've been planted
here to remind all of us of the long way home.

for Gustavo Pérez Firmat

from *In the Republic of Longing*

Bitterness

My father brings home the blood of horses on his hands,
his rough, calloused, thick-fingered hands; he comes home
from the slaughterhouse where the government places him to kill

old, useless horses that arrive from all over the island.
On his hands it comes, encrusted and etched into the prints
and wrinkles of his fingers, under his nails, dark

with the dirt too, the filth and grime, the moons of his fingers
pinked by its residue, his knuckles skinned from the endless work.
Sticky and sweet-scented is the blood of these horses,

horses to feed the lions in the new zoo that is moving
from Havana to Lenin's Park near where we live. Dark blood,
this blood of the horses my father slaughters daily, and loses

himself doing so. I, being a child, ask how many horses
it takes to feed a single lion. This, of course, makes my father
laugh. I watch as he scrubs and rinses dried blood from his

forearms and hands, those hands that kill the horses, the hands
that sever through skin and flesh and crush bone
because tough is the meat of old horses. Feed for the lions.

So my father, the dissident, the *gusano,* the Yankee lover, walks
to and from work on tired feet, with an aching body. He no longer
talks to anybody, and less to us, his family. My mother

and my grandmother, his mother. But they leave him alone,
to his moods, for they know what he is being put through.
A test of will. Determination. Salvation and survival.

My father, gloomy, under the new zoo tent on the grounds,
doesn't say much. He has learned how to speak with his hands.
Sharp are the cuts he makes on the flesh. The horses are shot

in the open fields, a bullet through the head, and are then
carted to where my father, along with other men, do the butchering.
He is thirty (the age I am now) and tired, and when he

comes home his hands are numb from all that chopping and sawing.
This takes place in 1969. Years later when we are allowed to leave
Havana for Madrid, to the cold winter of Spain, we find

ourselves living in a hospice. The three of us in a small room.
(My grandmother died and was buried in Havana.) Next door lives
a man named Izquierdo who wakes us with phlegmy coughs.

From our side of the clapboard walls, his coughing sounds
like thunder. We try to sleep; I try harder, but the coughing
seeps through and my father curses under his breath. I listen

to the heat as it tic-tacs through the furnace. My father tries
to make love to my mother. I try now not to listen.
The mattress springs sound like bones crushing.

My mother refuses without saying a word. This is the final time
she does so tonight. My father breaks the immense and inter-
minable silence, saying, "If you don't, I'll look for a Spanish

woman who will." Silence again, then I think I hear my mother
crying. "*Alguien,*" my father says, meaning someone, "will want
to, to . . ." (fuck him).

And I lay there on my edge of the mattress, sweat summoned
by the heat. My eyes are closed, and I listen hard, and then every
thing stops. This, I think, is a sound like death.

Then my father begins all over again. The room fills with small
noises . . . the cleaver falls and cuts through skin, tears
through flesh, crushes the bone, and then there is blood.

All that blood. It emerges and collects on slaughter tables,
the blood of countless horses. Sleep upon me, I see my father
stand by the sink in our Havana house patio. He scrubs and rinses

his hands. The blood whirls and dissolves slowly in the water.
Once again I summon the courage to go ahead and ask him how much
horse meat it takes to appease the hunger of a single lion.

Free

When we first arrived in the United States
from Franco's Spain, everything we encountered

or bought had "free" written on it.
The boxes of cereal spoke of a free mystery

surprise, the junk mail came bundled,
and somehow that word sang to us.

My father and I got wise—the word
became cheap, untrustworthy, hollow.

Having been fooled before, we knew what "free"
really meant. We learned lessons the hard way;

nothing free ever came so easily, but my mother—
who had heard stories of people throwing

out television sets, sofas, washing machines,
perfectly good chairs—believed in this land

of plenty where people discarded simply
because things were old or someone

had grown tired of them. She believed
in all that was cast to the curb. A cousin

who cruised the neighborhood streets
for these free goods told her of his finds

over the telephone. On the weekends,
she sent my father and me out to hunt,

to find these throwaways, but we always
came back empty-handed. We never

really looked. We stopped for donuts
or to watch a baseball game at the park.

Now, years later, my father dead, my mother
gets the mail, the catalogs, and she sends

it all up to me in Tallahassee, and she's circled
the word "free" and asks me what the deal is.

Most Sundays I try to convince her once
and for all that there are no deals, that nothing

is free, then there's silence over the line,
and I can hear her thinking otherwise.

She is a woman who wants to cling to something
as simple as a two-for-one deal, the extra, the much

more, *lo gratis:* these simple things she knows
have kept us going all these exiled years.

Gallos Finos

My father longed for the wild days of cockfighting
    in Cuban heat where he was born—the whiskey smell
        of the cocks' damp feathers, their slick smoothness,
    radiant flash in the bright sun—he knew too much
about the birds, their history, like how the Chinese

bred and crossbred the jungle fowl, *Gallus gallus,*
    with Himalayan Bankivas for lightning speed and flying,
        swift kicks, and with Malay birds for strength and wallop.
    They taught them the right skills of a fighter,
the punch, feint, roll, and *salto.* They marched them

through gamecock exercise, trimmed their blood-red wattles
    and combs, and stuffed dried chilies up their cloacas.
        A few thousand generations later in Cuba, the result
    was obvious in how to take two birds, program them
to kill each other, each a shimmered pulse of instinct,

training, and breeding, the dust from the pits rising—
    he loved that smell, my father, of when the birds eyed
        each other and charged—that moment of determined malice
    and viciousness, of these two roosters matched by weight,
given identical weapons attached to their cutoff bony

back spurs, knives or gaffs, razor-sharp, like curved
    ice picks, strapped onto their stumps—into an explosion of lost
        feathers, a flurry of beak and leg, a controlled anger,
    until the one bird remained standing, or fled, and the fight
came to an end, this pure act of endurance, like any other.

Cuban American Gothic

My father stands next to my mother,
both in the simple, stained work clothes

they wore to their factory jobs,
instead of sitting next to the Singer

overlap sewing machine, zippers
snaking all around her, she bends

in the background; beyond her a storm
rages, lightning fractures opaque skies,

while my father, instead of cutting
patterns for denim jeans, cradles an armful

of mason jars filled with blue fractal
light, bolts of lightning captured

for all time—in the distance, bad weather
so absolute, this rite of passage from their

immigrant lives—*la vida dura,* my father
calls it—this skeletal American landscape

exposed by lightning, this flash of longing,
as if by X-ray, in this new foreign town,

against the ravages of time and forgetting.

The Trouble with Frogs

It's irrational, I know, like the fear of flying
       or high places,
but irresistible nonetheless, for frogs hide
       in the luscious green
of the plantain's fronds. There, they nest
       and call out
for nuptial visitations, become invisible against
       the corrugated tin
of the outhouse at my grandmother's house,
       then jump. . . .
The neighborhood kids catch them and put them
       down my shirt
and in my pants. Who understands the terror
       of this cold and clammy
thing moving against the skin? At the time the child
       thinks there is no return
from such fear. At night beyond the mosquito net,
       they call out.
From Havana to Tallahassee,
       frogs have evolved
into this fear of a childhood not lived,
       not remembered,
but out there, in the distance, they call; they beckon
       no matter how far I travel;
I cannot escape this trouble with frogs.
       All I can do
is embrace the fact that they are there,
       like the past,
calling out, beckoning for the mind to leap.

A Song at the End of the Cuban Revolution

On the day Castro dies or flees
the *zun-zun* hovers
                    by the hibiscus flower,
the Russian boats on the harbor,
those that remain, sink to become reefs;
delighted, the manatee and cayman return,
the *tomeguines* and rainbow bunting nest in peace,
and the lizard will cease to change colors.

On the day of the end of the Cuban Revolution,
men, women, and children gather in the fields,
in the city streets, under the fallen propaganda,
torn banners and posters, the *güajiros* play
their *décimas* on their guitars. The *son* returns
to the island, the *maniceros* resume their chants.
The laughter of the maracas and the calling
of the *tumba* drums rise above all clatter
                    and human waking.

And those here and there who expect thunder
and the storm of vendettas are disappointed.
And those who expected bloodshed
                    are disappointed.
I do not believe it is occurring now.
As long as the cane and tobacco are in the fields,
as long as the Cuban parrots are nesting,
                    as long as children suckle,
everyone wants to believe it is happening now.

Only an ash-haired *babaláo,* prophet soothsayer,
never too busy to read his cowry shells,

repeats and translates what all those sounds
he is hearing mean:

There will be no better change in the world.
There will be no better change in the world.

from *Palm Crows*

Song to the *Cucuyo*

caught them at sundown in the tall grass
by the plantain plants by the porch

of our house in Havana, put several
in clear marmalade jars, brought them

inside the house, as pets, for the night;
there on the nightstand, in the dark,

they flashed their incendiary illuminations,
flashes of fluorescence, like faint lights

of a distant tarmac to signal the passing
of fears, such fears that keep children

awake for so long: old men in cold rooms
sit in the dark, stained undershirts,

the sound of phlegm, fingers gone yellow
from cigarette smoking. This long, long

road through distant cities, wrapped
in strange light. Everywhere, *cucuyos,*

from Havana to Tallahassee, to light
this child's way home.

Song to the Mango

For years while he lived in Los Angeles,
then later in Hialeah, Florida, my father
didn't eat mangos. He'd come home
from the market with my mother,
and he would tell her he'd seen them,
on the stands, mangos imported from Mexico,
flown from Hawaii, but he couldn't eat
them, not those mangos—it pained him,
he said, *"me duele mucho."* My friend
Wasabi once asked my father why,
they're just as good and sweet as Cubans,
and my father flew into a rage, called him a punk,
a blasphemer for making such a statement,
no mango could ever be as delicious
as a Cuban mango—we laughed
at my father's stubbornness, his refusal
to eat a fruit that he obviously loved,
because my mother claimed my father
dreamt of mangos; when a child he devoured
them by the dozen, their juices trickling
down his chin, their sweet tartness polished
on his lips, and when he died of a massive
heart attack at Palm Springs Hospital,
that day the mango fruit cocktail soured
in the cafeteria trays, nurses and doctors
who tasted it puckered in distaste, that night
I dreamt mangos fell off trees, plummeted
to the earth like shot ducks, dead hopes,
and I could finally understand my father's
avoidance, how even fruit too spoils
in foreign countries.

Song to the Passion Fruit

Everyday at noon when the noise
of the streets subsides, the lovers

come to this room, somewhere
in Old Havana, in this country

of lost causes, and they lie next
to each other on an *hamaca,*

a hammock he has strung up
by the window, low so that in it

their bodies resemble the shape
of a canoe, and their sunburned arms

as they dangle over the edge, oars.
They lie there and read what the cracks

on the walls say, these love poems
in peeling flecks of paint, truths

in the patches of damp ceiling tiles.
After lovemaking, they dream

their escapes where so much water
fills their being. A fly balances

itself on the lip of the water bowl,
braving slick porcelain smoothness;

the burning candle flickers in a moment
of breeze as it cries on itself, slowly,

slow like the lovers passing through
in this life. They love in this room,

silent, oblivious. All the while sparrows
have perched on the branches of the fruit

tree that grows on the balcony
outside the lovers' window.

A fruit tree, its knobby roots each day
deeper, twisted into the concrete and wire mesh,

grows up here on the third story balcony,
where sparrows now perch and preen.

Theirs is as much a history of this place
where the single fruit the tree has given

will suddenly be plucked by his arm
as it reaches out through the window

from the swing of the hammock. "This,"
he says, "is the fruit to quench our thirst.

The fruit to appease this hunger."
He brings this fruit to his lover, puts

it close to her mouth, watches as she takes
the first bite. Sweet is the juice of oblivion.

She now shares it with him—if they have
to pretend in this empty room,

then they will imagine this is part
of some story about to be told,

at the end of the end of the world
when the last two humans embrace,

seek consolation that like them, nature
has given, and given, a mother to all.

When the fruit is gone and the lovers
kiss, the fly plops into the water,

gives up its life for the sake of the magical.

Study in Shadow

In sepia, the stilted shadow of my father
      (the one taking the photograph?)
in Havana breaks where I stood
      next to the hibiscus, a boy of six,
hair scalloped back into the *Malanguita,*
      a proper boy's style, my mother's
favorite haircut for boys. This is 1968,
      outside the house of light, house
of shade, the world ablaze with protest,
      war, jungle orange poisons.
A smile faked for all time, my father urges
      it onto the lips of this spindly, awk-
ward boy—me—dressed in matched shirt
      and shorts, mother-sewed that summer,
clean, pretty, sadness riddled into my eyes.
      Our parrot Chícharo calls out:
"*Sonrisa!*" Smile, my father says behind
      the camera, then the flash of light
that swallows us both—all that remains
      of that boy is the squint of years,
the weight of memories, broken shadows
      of a man, his son, that life in Cuba,
bent on the grass, greener with possibility.

Nocturnal

I tapped your window with a key.
Nightly. After work. Sleepless

in Baton Rouge, the restlessness
a snake in my bones. You let me in.

We didn't speak to each other
there in the dark of your efficiency.

You took me by the hand and led
me. Naked, we loved

until the mattress crashed through
the frame and the next-door neighbor

banged for quiet, calling us sinners.
We kept silent and watched

the roaches, black dots that punctuated
our thoughts as they moved up the wall.

Within the hour I was dressed
and out the door, into the sultry

fog of a city, of a place, of this moment
in our lives. We met this way for months,

coiled into these trysts of lust.
Our body heat made condensation

on the windows. You wrote "don't"
with the tip of your finger. I looked

back long enough to see the woman
at the door, herself a creature driven

by the night to those places the heart
drives to ruin, to break hard against

so much longing, so much innocence.

Duende

In the torrential downpours, Lorca arrives one night
at our house. A particularly tempestuous night,
not only with the weather outside but with my father, inside.

My father, young then in Havana, Lorca's age when the great
poet was shot, is being driven to drink and madness
by his dissident government views, and Lorca glides

in from the porch shadows, not a drop of rain on him, not his
face nor his delicate hands. He leaves no mud prints
as he walks into our living room and sits on our worn chintz

sofa. What news have you of my father? my father asks the poet.
Lorca looks around, then lights a cigarillo; the incandescence
of the match's flame lights up his eyes. He exhales, then says:

"He died thrown from his horse." True, my father says and runs
into another room. I approach slowly, driven by the smell
of brilliantine in the poet's combed hair. "Tell me about

duende, Señor Lorca." He smiles and aims a puff of smoke
at me—it makes my eyes water. "You think you have it, *Niño?*"
he asks. "I don't know," I say. I need the trembling

of this moment, then silence. . . . "If you ever leave
this forsaken country," he adds, "you will neither sing
nor play music. But the *duende* will haunt you, like this memory

of me, sitting here." Twenty-five years from today, you will
live in Tallahassee, Florida, and it too will be raining.
I will knock on your door. You will let me in, and I will come

and sit on your couch. You will ask me what news have I
of your father, and I will say: "He is where you last left him,
on a hospital bed, dead of a massive coronary." You will say

how useless. I will say: "*Aprende,* the guitars are weeping.
Hear them?" We will sit in silence and listen to the rain pour
down on the earth. Poet in crinoline, you come from remote

regions of sorrow and return to the labyrinth: love, crystal,
stone, you vanish down the rivers of the earth to the sea.

In the House of White Light

When my grandmother left the house
        to live with my aunts, my grandfather,

who spent so much time in the sugar-
        cane fields, returned daily to the emptiness

of the clapboard house he built
        with his own hands, and he sat in the dark

to eat beans he cooked right in the can.
        There in the half-light he thought of all he'd lost,

including family, country, land; sometimes
        he slept upright on that same chair,

only stirred awake by the restlessness
        of his horse. One night during a lightning

storm, my grandfather stripped naked
        and walked out into the fields around

the house saying "*que me parta un rayo,*"
        may lightning strike me, and he stood

with his arms out; the hard rain pelted
        his face, and then the bolts fell

about him, and he danced and cradled
        these filaments in his arms, but they

kept falling, these flashes of white light,
        and he ran back inside and brought out

an armful of large mason jars my grandmother
        used for pickling, and he filled them

with fractal light. Like babies, he carried
        the jars inside and set them all about the house,

and the house filled with the immense
        blinding light that swallowed everything,

including the memories of how each nail
        sunk into the wood, the water level rose

in the well, the loss of this country,
        the family who refused to accept him now,

that in this perpetual waking, the world
        belonged to those who believed in the power

of electricity, those moments zapped
        of anguish, isolation, this clean and pure

act of snatching lightning out of heavy air,
        plucking lightning like flowers from a hillside.

The Great Chinese Poets Visit Havana

Imagine Tu Fu and Li Po as they have come
    to the island to lecture on the beauty of rice,

the calligraphy of desire, the way a bamboo
    quill shivers in their hands as ink saturates

their longing. They have come to speak
    about the Art of Repetition to other Chinese

who escaped communism in China only
    to relive it here in Cuba. The poets look out

at the waves beyond *El malecón,* the seawall
    against which the waves spill their secrets.

They witness the *balseros,* so many Cuban rafters
    waving good-bye, *adiós,* as they become mere dots

on the horizon, like characters on the paper.
    Here the egret flaps its wing at the cayman,

at the submerged manatee. The river flows
    beyond the dilapidated buildings, a poetry

of crumbling stone; a mango tree grows
    on a third story balcony where birds

perch against this air of parting. They come
    to read the letters being sent from home, read

them and weep, a fluttering of words against
    the faintest of breezes, like the thinnest of papers.

Listen, they travel the island, they witness the resilience,
      they call out for inner strength in the face of scarcity,

their sweet voices rise and echo over Sierra Maestra,
      the sullen, distraught faces of so many birds do not

honor them, these great men who merely come
      to speak this cryptic language of absence and longing.

El Exilio

> White birds over the gray river.
> Scarlet flowers on the green hills.
> I watch the Spring go by and wonder
> if I shall ever return home.
>
> Tu Fu

After his accident in Hialeah where he worked
    as a coffee packer, my father returned home
from the hospital and sat by the window
    of the room where my mother sewed,
and he watched the world through the two-inch
    window bars, *mi prisión,* he called it,
this catatonia of spirit, he sighed,
    breathing with difficulty in the air-
conditioned apartment he shared with my mother,
    and we'd talk on the phone once during
the week, and then on Sundays, he spoke little
    of how he felt, often repeating yesterday's
news or how gray the weather hovered in Miami,
    these cumulus clouds of surrender, a bad
omen for those crossing the Florida Straits on make-
    shift rafts, all trying to get to freedom,
and my father would chuckle his ironic laugh over
    the telephone line as if to say few made it,
and indeed when they made it, *pa' que,* he'd say,
    to lose life in the United States, too much
work, not enough money, too little to show for it,
    but he believed in freedom, in how he came
and went out of his house and not a soul
    asked him for papers or where he was going,
like his old life in Cuba, and the language,
    El Inglés, he never learned, only chewed
on a few necessary words like "mortgage,"

"paycheck," "punch clock," "bills," . . .
the rest all sounded like the barks of mad
         dogs in an alleyway, the rest sounded
like the poetry he lacked in spirit; *El Exilio*
         he sighed, did this to him, his life,
and my mother would sew a dress's hem,
         and she'd stop long enough to tell him
he was wrong, their (our?) lives here
         had been a blessing, even if hard,
even if they were now alone in this apartment
         in Hialeah where my father watched
the children arrive in the yellow buses
         at the school across the street;
he was there when they came and there when
         they left, his visions of a daily routine,
like clockwork, beyond the barred window,
         his sedentary life without the use
of his hands, and often, he looked at his thin
         fingers and thought of the crows he ran
over by the roadside in Cuba, when younger,
         when he knew bad luck when he saw it,
the way these scavengers of the earth
         flocked over a rotting carcass of a killed
animal, the way he wanted to scream out
         his bad luck in English now, say "Fuck You!"
to his life, to this life of sitting and watching.
         The steeling of his heart.

The Stayer

Simply, my uncle Chicho stayed
       back in Cuba, against the family's
advice, because everyone left

       and he chose to stay, and this act
of staying marked him as "crazy"
       with most of the men, and he stayed

there in a shack behind my aunt's
       clapboard house, sat in the dark
of most days in the middle

       of the packed-dirt floor and nodded
at the insistence of light, the way
       it darted through holes in the tin

roof where the rain drummed
       like the gallop of spooked horses.
This is where he was born, he chanted

       under his breath to no one, why should
he leave, live in perpetual longing
       within exile? He learned long ago

to count the passing of time
       in how motes danced in the shaft
of white light, the *chicharras* echoed

       their trill against the emptiness
of life, against the wake of resistance
       in this place he knew as a child,

as a man, *un hombre* bent against this idea
     of leaving his country, call him *loco*.
What nobody counted on was that answers

        come only to those who sit in the quiet
of their own countries, tranquil
       in the penumbra, intent on hearing the song

of a *tomeguín* as it calls for a mate
       to come nest in the shrubs out there,
while in here, he witnesses how light

fills the emptiness with the meaning of stay.

from *Banyan*

Cancionero del Banyan

The wind frustrates itself, held
in its oval leaves, sifted

through tendril, ropelike
roots of the mighty banyan,

stumps of elephant feet, tough
gray skin. This tree doesn't bend

against strong wind or hurricane.
This one survived Andrew

in Coral Gables, where the Cubans
live now. Like sons, they grow

backward into the ground, sprout
more trunks. Eternal. How like exile

to leave such marks on these spots,
these places where life continues

in exile, a father's hand clutching
any dirt it can call its own.

Beyond a Street Corner in Little Havana

Waiting for you might be a mallet, a blow
　　　to the temple, an embrace, a kiss,
a scream, bad breath, *un cafecito,* freshly
　　　brewed, lotto tickets (lucky you),

a vendor of *mamoncillos,* lemons, mangos,
　　　maní tostado, a flung decapitated white
dove from a second story window, a potted
　　　bonsai of *guayaba,* a pig's squeal as it darts

around an apartment, children tugging at its tail,
　　　a parrot that sings *"Cuando salí de Cuba,"*
your father's face captured in death, eyes
　　　winking in the peeling paint . . . this life

is yours and only yours, these grim memories
　　　of returning, a savage smile, red like innards,
a fruitless search for all past, a woman gone,
　　　not your mother, but she calls your name;

turn toward her, your own shadow mocks
　　　you, splinters away; yes, this is your
life at this corner, open your eyes, crank-start
　　　desire—you've come a long way. Now rain

falls, sleets downward from the awnings;
　　　stay put, say greetings, this is your life
　　　blown backward.

No Work Poem #1

what hurt my father most after his accident
where one bad turn to the water fountain
nearly cost him his life, a forklift dropped
a pallet of 526 pounds of compressed card-
board on him and crushed him like a bug,
was how the company told all his work friends
that because my father had gotten a lawyer
they couldn't talk to my father anymore,
that it was policy that no one come in close
contact with him as though he had malaria
or some other contagious disease. My father
was depressed by this, a man who shared hard
work with other men, and they were his friends,
and his true friends came by anyway to share
stories of what went on at work, and this helped
rehabilitate my father, slowly, and I saw it
in his eyes when his best friend, Manzano,
told my father how many fewer boxes of coffee
they packed without him, that my father,
el campeón, still held the record—I didn't
understand this kind of work-talk,
but I saw how my father when he thought
he was alone would raise his hands and look
at them in the light, as though they were gifts,
and they were; with his hands he worked,
hard, with his hands, he beat the clock,
with his hands he provided for his family,
and proud, he looked at them, the way his
thin fingers now moved; with his hands
he clawed at life, what is given, what is taken.

Mango Eating in America

The best way to eat a mango,
my father-in-law once told me,
is in the shower, how juices

run down your chin
and neck, when the seed slips
out of your hands like soap,

and you bite down on the soft
meat of a delicious, ripe mango,
and I remember the times I went

into the mango orchards of a distant
neighborhood, climbed the trees,
shook a branch or two, knocked

down an armful of mangos, then sat
to eat them on the stairs of a house
previously owned by a doctor

who'd left his country, and there
in the quiet, between the chirps
of birds and the warm, sticky breeze,

I ate the mangos, bit into them
with a hunger for sweetness,
wondered about a god who created

such a delicious tropical fruit,
so perfect, and the trees loomed
around me like these giants,

friends offering up their gifts;
it's been years now since I've eaten
a real Cuban mango, but the memory

comes back not only in dreams,
but in Miami when the street vendors
lift their bags of three mangos

for a dollar, and I am so tempted,
but decline the offer because I know
that, like my father who never ate imported

mangos again in his life, I will one day soon.

for Denise Duhamel & Nick Carbó

Recitative after Rembrandt's "The Anatomy Lesson of Dr. Nicolaes Tulp"

how the whiteness of flesh beckons the doctor's eyes averted
from the flash of muscle, tendon like pulleys, rubber
bands useless now in death, and in the brightest light,

the good doctor's hands shine, one holding a pair of tweezers,
the other in explanatory gesture as if to say look how the red
of exposed arteries, darkened in crimson light, contrasts

against corpse-pale, moments when corporeal secrets
still held the curiosity of those gathered to study how the body
works, functions, even in this futility of the laid-out, another

corpse donated by the city morgue, a drunkard, a wayward soul,
and I think of my own father, a hard-working man, dead
of complications in surgery, or rather, how a blood clot choked

his heart into submission, and his eyes closing to the world,
a fluorescence of white doves aflutter on the roof of a train
station, my father a young man of fifteen on the way to Havana

to seek his fortunes, and fifty years later, in another country,
in the bark of a foreign tongue, in the whirlwind of exile,
his ears surrender to the sound of a muted cry, his own,

and the hospital's ICU doctors and nurses flock to him, his heart
will not start up again, and they paddle it with electricity, paddle
again, but his heart knows its calling, a royal palm tree

calls it home, where the rivers teem with the silver of fish,
fiery beings under the water's mirror, and he wants to go home,
he yearns for this place of his youth, the doctors and nurses

stand dumbfounded because Dr. Tulp, despite a lifetime
of practice and a steady hand, is too late; science has failed him,
my father, as science fails us all.

The Table

After my father-in-law died
of lung cancer, my mother said
the table was down to three legs,

and I thought it funny until my father
died of a massive coronary caused
by a post-surgery blood clot,

when she said we were now down
to two, and now my mother-in-law
fights lymphatic cancer, third round

treatment, and my mother wipes
the table top clean each time
after dinner, and I can't help

but think of her table analogy,
and those times at a café or restaurant
when you sit there, elbows on the table,

and you notice it's a little wobbly
so you fold a couple of napkins
into a wad and prop up the short leg,

and I can see it in my mother's eyes,
this idea of a table, just the top, legless,
a piece of wood on the floor, useless

now in the face of so much passing.

from *Guide to the Blue Tongue*

La tempestad de las palabras blancas

In this island, the saying goes, *cuando llueve,*
llueve a cántaros. The villagers prepare

by simply tying everything down, thatched
hut roofs; animals, pet parrots are brought

inside. When the storm surges inland, Calibán
studies it from inside his own hut. Three days

of rain now gush down from angry skies;
even the frogs drown hidden in the *V*s of plantain

fronds, hushed in their final hour of surrender.
No respite, even for the quiet, the broken, the ugly

like this man on a hammock, under a leaking roof,
his life like all these leaks, seeping away, hour

by hour, this lamentation of those island-bound,
not even this physical storm can piece together,

cuando un hombre quiere a una mujer, the wind
blows out the candles, hushes the living's despair.

At night the wind hums through bamboo shutters,
bangs a door or two shut, opens cupboards,

rattles ancient china. In his chest, he hears thunder,
this restless gallop of stallions broken in, *domados.*

En las tinieblas de la noche, el corazón se espanta.

Prospero's Papermaking Recipe

when making the paper, never talk, good paper is made
　　in complete quietness of the mind　　a fly buzzes trapped in a lamp shade

hands and fingers spread the pulp evenly,
　　the act is in total rhythm with the body　　　　　　　　a hummingbird
　　　　　　　　　　　　　　　　　　　　　　　　　　　pierces a flower

left hand picks up the *su* (bamboo mat)　　　the children dream of
　　　　　　　　　　　　　leaves fallen backward
　　　　　　　　　　　　　　　onto the branches

when releasing the *su*, hold it at a 90-degree angle
　　　　to avoid making bubbles　　　　　　　　breath is the first wind
　　　　　　　　　　　　　　　　　of a storm

hold the *geta* (wood papermaking mold) with a tiger grip,
　　　but with a flexible hand and wrist that follows

　　　　　　　　　the motion　　a bucket falls into a deep well,
　　　　　　　　　　　　　　　its sound echoes,
　　　　　　　　　　　a tympanum of rung bells

birds flocked on the rice fields scattershot heavenward,
　　　when they reach the clouds　the paper, the world,
　　　　　　　　　　　　　　　complete.

The Alchemy of Self-Implosion

Once the filament breaks in the heart,
like in a lightbulb, you cannot repair it.

Blood stops dead on its tracks. A glass
house cannot withstand the weight

of a lover's breath. It crumbles with desire
and cannot be resurrected from the ashes

of the forsaken. It is an inward spiral,
shards of longing like forget-me-nots

trampled by spotted horses out to graze.
Wood burns unevenly. His eyes close finally,

a curtain drawn to keep out light,
configured to puzzle even surgeons.

A mitral valve cannot be coaxed by shock,
no electric current works at revival.

All that remains is for the hand to plunge
to the heart, rip it out, and massage it.

It becomes a divining rod held backward,
pointed at a crescent moon; black crows flock

into oblivion, eclipse this life's sun.

Prospero in Havana

Given to bouts of melancholia, the tempest-raiser
spends time in the garden, picking hibiscus

with the gentlest touch of his fingers, unsteady
in this old age, arthritic, eyes burned-on-the-page

from so much reading, the old books stacked
around the walls of his clapboard shack, the poets

come from all over the island to borrow paper,
which the old man makes for them, recycles,

the vats of paper pulp fertile breeding ground
for the mosquitos that bite his thin exposed legs;

the wounds fester from his constant scratching.
He misses his daughter, and at night he sighs

and curses the darkness. By candlelight he reads
his ancient texts, tries to find order in the minute,

the mundane. The natives call him *El mago blanco*
because of his paper magic, the way he watches

the storms roll inland, like an illusion of dream,
from chaos to creation, from reality to realization,

this *tempestas* of time, how he can make seconds flow
as sand dropping backward into the hourglass,

to be possessed, this alchemy of desire so far, so near.

The Reconciliation Between
Los que se fueron y los que se quedaron

It's an old story in this Caribbean island, how some leave
and others stay. What is exchanged between the villagers?

This gift of words. A storm or two. In the old man's books,
the story has to do with a man who fell from his roof, fell

to pieces, and when the dictator's horses, and the dictator's
men couldn't put *el hombre* back together again, the children

gathered at the lip of the beach to lay down hibiscus blossom
wreaths. This is true of the story of the man who fell out

of the sky, the great revolutionary man, who crashed in a Cessna,
and now schoolchildren sing songs to him, or the Argentinian

who spoke many languages, who had been a medical student
in Buenos Aires, who came to this island to fight for freedom.

Where is he now? When the *zun-zun* hovers above a trough
filled with rainwater, we know it will rain for decades; those

who left will miss their homeland, those who stayed will say
there is no return. Only the dead know the truth. One day

everyone will come together, that's true—for now, we wait,
wait out this rain between the shores of exile. While we wait,

we love, eat, drink; our children grow up knowing the difference
between here and there. They will return one day and plant

new trees, replace what history's tempest has blown away.

Curved Geometry, a Botero Beauty's Retrospective

A chrysanthemum flower in the hair. Who could resist?
Blatant, such excess of flesh, so talcum-powder white,

cartography of curves, mounds really, concupiscence,
derelict pleasures, this delight in so much rotundity.

Eros in bed, braided hair, small eyes, lips, breasts.
Forged lovemaking on such a small bed, a simple test.

Gigantism this isn't, but simply nothing like Giacometti,
handsome Matador, red cape flung over the bedpost

inviting the bull's charge (*Olé Toro!*). Goya's proud *Maja,*
juicy portraits, round, well filled, a shape that needs filling?

Kindred spirits, lovers, difficulty in kowtowing, portly.
Lathered ladies in bathtubs filled with soapy scented waters.

Macho men with penciled mustaches, cherubic faces,
narcotic smiles, cigarettes so cool in their thin lips.

Obsidian smooth skin, so much of it, the eye fills slowly.
Parasols in the park, below them gauzy-dressed ladies,

quiverful of a hint of sex in the afternoon air, flirtatious,
rakishly gorgeous, smart, funny, yearning for a heavy-set

smoocher, someone as interested in round shapes as they.
Tantamount to this dimpled geometry, a jiggle of thighs.

Undulant but inviting, yes, luringly embellished by garters.
Virginal some, others dubious, of course, completely jealous.

Wanton needs, who could possess them? Here, a woman
xylophonist by trade, graceful in the way she plays and plays.

You want to possess them, their perfumed bodies, hair,
zipper them open, their hot lips, inviting us to taste, savor.

Isla

In Los Angeles I grew up watching *The Three Stooges,*
The Little Rascals, Speed Racer, and the Godzilla movies,

those my mother called *"Los monstruos,"* and though I didn't
yet speak English, I understood why such a creature would,

upon being woken up from its centuries-long slumber, rise
and destroy Tokyo's buildings, cars, people—I understood

by the age of twelve what it meant to be unwanted, exiled,
how you move from one country to another where nobody

wants you, nobody knows you, and I sat in front of the TV,
transfixed by the snow-fizz on our old black and white,

and when Godzilla bellows his eardrum-crushing growl,
I screamed back, this victory-holler from one so rejected

and cursed to another. When the monster whipped its tail
and destroyed, I threw a pillow across my room; each time

my mother stormed into the room and asked me what,
what I thought I was doing throwing things at the walls.

"¡Ese monstruo, esa isla!" she'd say. That monster, that island,
and I knew she wasn't talking about the movie. She meant

her country, mine, that island in the Caribbean we left behind,
itself a reptile-looking mass on each map, on my globe,

a crocodile-like creature rising again, eating us so completely.

for Jarret Keene

At the Somnambulists' Convention

where once a year the usual complaints are voiced:
the sound of ambulance and fire truck sirens,
car alarms set too sensitive, barks of distant
yard dogs, ticktock of windup clocks, whack-
whack of police helicopters on the chase,
a dripping faucet, gurgling toilets, pipes'
hiss, heavy-breathing wives, snorers really,
bad weather, static of telephone lines, buzz
of computer equipment left on like a dead
whisper from beyond . . . me? Silence
is the root of my insomniac ways, my girls
asleep in the room down the hallway,
and how I know there are teenage boys
in Mexico waiting for them, in dirty rooms,
how they'd love to have them, speak
with their tongues in their ears, and I stay
up most nights like a guardian, hell's
sentinel, a mad dog chasing its tail,
and I say they will not get them, those men;
my daughters, I keep vigil by their bedroom
door and watch over their sleep, how soundly
they sleep; those men, they will still be there . . .
in Mexico, here, everywhere, waiting.
Little do they know I pass through their nights
like a freight train loaded with radioactive
cargo, and I burn, shine in their malice, glow.

Shakespeare Visits Havana

When asked how he arrived, he pointed a red finger
    toward the docks in Regla beyond El Malecón,

where the dockworkers spilled like ants out of the bellies
    of ships, sacks and boxes on their shoulder, and he

said he'd come because he'd heard of the great coffee,
    cigars, sugar so sweet . . . and in his old age, like one

of his greatest old men, Prospero, he wanted to feel
    the Caribbean lunar bliss, the sway of palm frond

against his face, the scent of gardenia and jasmine.
    In the streets he walked as children played and men

drank in the penumbra of *bodegas* with other men,
    aguardiente, firewater, and he felt so fertile he couldn't

wait to sit down and commit word to paper, say
    the world doesn't stop, not here in this island of fire

where the sun bleaches everything, enough joy
    to fill the hearts of men, and women, the beautiful

ones standing on the wrought iron veranda balconies,
    an *abanico* in their delicate hands, maidens all.

Later, in his room, he will open the sea-facing windows,
    take a deep breath of the fresh salt air and sigh,

a memory of homeland a stone's weight in his chest,
        and he thinks he understands what it is to live in exile,

self inflicted, no less, like the one Hemingway knew,
        Wallace Stevens, Stephen Crane, and others, always

there will be others who will arrive, breathe in the air,
        and succumb to deepest melancholia; at his desk

he will write *Shakespeare* and pronounce it in Spanish
        for the first time, the words like hummingbirds

drinking the sweet nectar from his lips, a kiss of remembrance.

The Old Soothsayer Enters Santiago de Cuba

Teiresias, what caused your blindness at seven?
How you unfurled your fingers, showed men

a glimpse of their rotten hearts, a globule, a seed,
this memory of desire from having seen Athene.

"*Esa mujer sabrosa,*" you would have said. "*Linda.*"
But she splashed water into your eyes, this poison

of the ages, how you would never be able to look
at rivers, mountains, a gardenia's yellow blush.

Upon entering this island of fire, your words
turn to *décimas guajira,* a mynah bird's squawk

upon the lips of men who won't believe you,
a plague of lies in their lives, enough to destroy

them in their minds. Follow the scent
of sea foam; it will lead you home, deeper still

in this land of constant lack. A burden so heavy,
most men cannot bring themselves to hear you.

At seventy, another woman wipes your eyes
with chamomile tea, rubs your boyish chest

as if she knew that in order for men to save
themselves, their country, they must suffer thus.

Sure, you will live a long life, a bloody path
in the wake of so much strife, so much melancholia,

but you pass through with a wicked, sharp tongue.

American Drag Rhapsody: J. Edgar Hoover in Havana

He always came to the Tropicana Night Club in Old Havana,
a touch of Yves St. Laurent perfume behind the ears; a contact
would meet him there and then take him to the underground

gay nightclubs, where the free-for-all made his head spin,
after the *mojitos,* and all the bump-and-grind action he'd go
home with the blond who caressed his face with smooth dove-

feather hands, tickled him on the soft backs of his knees, licked
him there where the sultry Cuban men liked to give *la espuela,*
a trick they learned from the French, that much he was sure

of—Ah, those nights in Havana, those young men who knew him
better than his own mother. Music pulsing behind stucco walls,
a light glinting off a chandelier . . . these nights of release

from daily tensions. The games he played. His favorite scene
of any movie was Ava Gardner's scene with the two dark
and handsome boys in *Night of the Iguana,* shot in Acapulco.

He liked this bite-squeeze of flesh, no doubt. One night
he painted his lips bright red, put on a flamenco dress, sunset
red, white polka dots the size of quarters on the ruffles, onyx shiny

pumps, and he danced in front of mirrors; some distant guitar
weep and clatter of castanets helped him keep the rhythm. Nobody
knew him at the Havana Hilton, not here, not there at the clubs.

He loved this anonymity, this disappearing act of vanishing
before mirrors. Silk scarves around his neck, cotton blouses
rubbing against his nipples. Oh those glorious Havana

mornings when he opened the windows to let some light sneak in:
people below on the move, the bakery boys coming in to work
the dough with their rough fingers, pigeons on the wires, a man

on a balcony with a cigarette in his mouth, smoke wisping
in the wind. Holy Evanescence. How many mornings like this
would he have left in the world? How many nights would he feel

this rapture of passion, unbridled, free? The young man behind
him embracing him to greet the day like lovers, the way men
have held each other into an eternity.

New Poems

Indigo Bunting's Last Molt

in this island of   twisted branch,
     to which you return to change

into new dress: blustering indigo, ice blue,
that blinding color
         of perilous crossings

where nobody knows your name
other than *mariposa* / butterfly-bird.

What secrets do your falling feathers
     reveal of places whose names

     better remain unspoken?

Here among this verdant promise
of new beginnings, transform

into a dagger, a cold-steel scalpel
with which to slice the heavens,

     slatted light now piercing
        through rain clouds.

The wind knows   the sound of your
passing all too well;
       it hears secret

     codes in the flutter of your wings.
Return now from exile changed,

and move on knowing only the breath-
     taking blueness of this life.

The Exile Speaks

of a red tongue, black words,
a necessary longing for shadow,

a corpuscle, a dangled leaf
from a spiderweb's thread,

useless hands; fingers claw
any dirt; seeds bloom into fists,

an anger never allowed to ebb,
dreams of rotted, worm infested

pulp, all that tastes bitter, *agrio*
like bile, a regurgitation of lost

steps. Why not forget? Teeth
chatter in cold night air, dentures

in a glass. Away from the mouth,
teeth sing to all those about to drown.

Poem for Eliades Ochoa,
Maestro del alambre dulce

You make the trees sing in your fingers, Cuba's
landscape comes alive through the pick & twang

of your instrument's strings—the oxen-pulled cane
carts, the *guajiro*'s sombrero to keep out the harsh

light of the sun, royal palms bent against the ravages
of the storm, "*Ayer salió Josefina a buscar un buen*

caldero, un caldero para tostar un buen café . . ."
Hills, verdant valleys, a brook, endless pasture lands,

the bronze of neighing horses, how you make music
out of wood, string, this plucking of chords, zing

in rhythm with the *clave, guayo,* and *maracas.*
Décimas guajiras, the music of *yerba buena,* healing.

Bridge between two long and interminable distances.

La Florida

Lugubrious days pass with the amplitude of manatees,
hibiscus unfold their smiling vortex to confused bees,

somewhere near Turkey Point a crocodile grows a foot
by the day, tourists mistake the big ones for logs,

anhingas play Jesus on the Spanish moss-riddled branches
of oaks and junipers, crucified in the sun. Feral Quaker

parrots build nests high up in the banyan trees. Orchids,
capuchin monkeys loosed from an animal distributor

warehouse, memories of the bearded lady and the lizard
man, retired now in Palatka, holding court in the shade

of a parasol by their trailer. Russian midgets, rockets
shot into the eye of the moon, this magic of fireflies

zapping their phosphorescence in the night air, jasmine,
gardenia—somewhere a man barbecues 4-inch-thick steaks

in a thing called the Green Egg. A firefighter, a player
of handball. When his son visits once a year from Vegas

he asks when will he return to Tampa, his home. Who isn't
lured by so much sun, heat? The permanence of weather—

or by the mystery of sun showers when the sky opens up
and pelts the earth with a momentary lapse of crying.

Right now, somewhere in the Everglades, a fish jumps
out of the water and into the mouth of an alligator.

Nobody's there to witness it, but it happens again and again.

Japanese Magnolia

its crimson lips open to blush this pure
act of defiance against the morning chill,

frost a blanket on the grass where spiders
have built canopies in pockets everywhere,

some between the petals of this magnolia.
A place to catch the next meal or lay eggs?

A mockingbird, confused by such display
of flower, invisible spiderweb, belts out

a song, then flies against the first opened
flower, plucks one petal, then flies off—

Wherever it drops this petal, a fist grows,
in it the red tendrils of fingers, fire tongues;

what is spoken becomes a white moth
unfurling its wings, fluttering this cryptic

language the earth telegraphs from one
creature to another, of all things ravished.

The Seed Collector

My father, for all the years he lived in exile,
spent afternoons, after he arrived from work,

slicing open pomegranates, *guayaba,* mangos,
eating of their meaty pulp, then saving the seeds.

He dried them on napkins held down by rocks
on the brick fence post, or he placed them

in plates and left them to dry in the wind
by the open kitchen window. Once I asked

what he was doing with all these seeds, and he
spoke of the rarer fruits we didn't have here

in Los Angeles, the *guanabana,* the *mamey,*
mamoncillo, and *caimito* . . . fruit I remember

eating back in my Cuban childhood, but never
again, and he missed them, he said. *Las extraño.*

He dried the seeds of bonnet peppers, red,
green, *ají de cachucha,* tomato seeds, habanero

chilis . . . seeds like teeth in the sun. Why
so many? And he'd stick a hand deep in his

pockets and show me a handful of them,
these seeds like gold crumbs in his hands—

He scattered them everywhere as he walked,
on people's yards, in his own, on the medians,

sidewalks, open fields, vacant lots. His mission
was to plant these seeds along his path, a memory

of his days in Cuba, our days in paradise, he said
and walked out of the house toward the setting sun.

The Burning

Where this idea for burning
    cane fields came from, my father
        told me once, perhaps Louisiana,

where, as in Cuba, between
    the rough swaths of leaves on sugar-
        cane stalks and the heat, nobody

wanted to cut the cane, so the fire
    started, and I would sit there
        on my aunt's lap and watch

the fields burning. I thought
    of these great tongues of flame
        lapping the night sky. Memory's

fingers trying to reach upward
    toward some meaning, something
        that spoke of how fire, cane, man

came to be so connected in this land
    of endless sugarcane fields, mills.
        In the morning, among smoldering

wisps of smoke, the men entered,
    their machetes in hand, their straw
        hats on their heads, crow-black boots

on their feet. They wrapped bandannas
round their mouths and disappeared
into these blackened mouths that called

out to them. Children of fire, of ash.

for Jack Bedell

Tea Leaves, *Caracoles,* Coffee Beans

My mother, who in those Havana days believed in divination,
found her tea leaves at *El Volcán,* the Chinese market/apothecary,

brought the leaves in a precious silk paper bundle, unwrapped
them as if unwrapping her own skin, and then boiled water

to make my dying grandmother's tea; while my mother read
its leaves, I simply saw *leaves floating* in steaming water,

vapor kissed my skin, my nose became moist as a puppy's.
My mother did this because my grandmother, her mother-in-law,

believed in all things. Her appetite for knowledge was vast,
the one thing we all agreed she passed down to me, the skinny

kid sent to search for *caracoles,* these snail shells
that littered the underbrush of the empty lot next door.

My mother threw them on top of the table, cleaned them of dirt,
kept them in a mason jar and every morning before breakfast,

read them on top of the table, their way of falling, some up,
some down, their ridges, swirls of creamy lines, their broken

edges. . . . Everything she read looked bad, for my grandmother,
for us, for staying in our country, this island of suspended

disbelief. My mother read coffee beans too, with their wrinkled,
fleshy green and red skin. Orange-skinned beans she kept aside.

Orange meant death, and my mother didn't want to accept it.
I learned mostly of death from the way a sparrow fell

when I hit it in the chest with my slingshot and a lead pellet
I made by melting my toy soldiers. The sparrow's eyes

always hid behind droopy eyelids, which is how my grandmother
died, by closing her eyes to the world; truth became this fading

light, a tunnel, as everybody says, but instead of heaven
she went into the ground, to that one place that still nourishes

the tea leaves, *caracoles,* and the coffee beans, which, if I didn't
know better, I'd claim shone; those red-glowing beans

in starlight were the eyes of the dead looking out through
the darkness as those of us who believed in such things walked

through life with a lightness of feet, spirit, a vapor-aura
that could be read or sung.

Orange

Carved on the lip of this crow-black river,
    our names, the searchers, of brown skin,
waiting under the shade of orange-heavy
    trucks, canals infested with this memory
of leaden clouds, endless orange groves. . . .

Sunday of damnation, how one gnarled
    hand plucks this bitter fruit from trees,
another reminder of why, why we got kicked
    out, but his is no garden, *amigo,* what's
shaken is never split into equal portions.

The Haves have more, the Have-nots, less.
    Sun upon the rock, water, a turtle crosses
the street only to get squashed, serves up
    its life to the vultures, these solitary monks.
The lights on the house on the hill come on.

There's a woman carrying a baby on her back.
    A red bandanna covers her mouth to keep dust
out. A group of men drinking beer outside
    Pancho's call out to her, but she ignores them.
She knows who they are, she knows what they

are good for. No difference between her feet
    and the dirt she walks on. The baby will learn
to see orange, dream of oranges. At night
    the moon will be mother orange. The sun,
well, father fire from which all earthly hues

borrow their names. We are here in the middle
of the middle of midnight. Even now, on this
moonless night, the golden orbs hung from trees
shine, release their bittersweet essence into air.
The air carries it for free, as it's learned to do.

all die, why not drown in our own
words, our tongues rolling back
into our throats to reach happy notes.

Virgil's Crib

Here the toe-chewed marionette,
tufts of teddy-bear stuffing cobwebbed
into the corner rails from which young

Virgil screamed, "Get me out of here,"
his grandmother's dentures, stolen
again, hard under his pillow. They

chatter to him at night from Sappho's
love poems. A *murcielago* mobile
dangles shadows across the moonlit

walls, sheets of paper devouring
the vastness of light . . . embroidered
pillow with Woody Woodpecker's

red crest, which turns the boy on.
At night, after everyone falls asleep,
the young gunslinger shoots ghosts

of the people he'll never know, duck-
gallery style. Once during a bout
with chicken pox the boy draws

his words on the sheet with scabs
of infested wounds, on his body now
this pockmarked history of what he said.

The What of Rocks

Everywhere I travel I stop to pick up a rock,
a hard-kept promise to my mother who needs
the foundation of hard things in my life,
some certainty at my hand. So I walk, keep
my eye on the ground—a red-ticked pebble
here, an ochre-hued, polished stone there.
I gather them at night in darkness; only
then do they feel smooth enough to carry
back. They are the eyes of my father
in moonlight. I want to say rocks know
the truth about a wicked tongue. Some,
and I know this is far-fetched, blink
at me, wink as if in approval. "Pick me,"
says the one near the tree. "I weigh
nothing, for in me is the hollow air you
need." A rock held in the night does feel
as light as a dead father, a tongue gone dry,
a mouth so thirsty for words that when
you say "rock," something grounds you
to the spot, though it could simply be
the earth mistaking you for its own hunger.

Upon Hearing that My Poetry Is Being Published "Everywhere"

Outside, a flock of buzzards communes
over a possum's carcass, monks in prayer,
except for the malcontent who bats

onyx wings against emptiness and rejection.
A cardinal blasts his mating call, unseen
by the indigo snake coiling up a branch

to reach the sun. Duckweed overruns
the pond's surface, becomes sludge
in the first days of frost—a mint Slurpee,

one of my girls calls it. Somewhere
someone picks up the Bible in a motel room,
finding comforting words of damnation,

a man shaving at the bathroom sink,
his image multiplying before him because
he is looking at himself on a mirror

facing a door mirror. He shaves again,
and again. Grows younger, turns
into that boy who looked into a puddle

to find himself turned into an amaranth,
this flower of constant and eternal
blooming. If I turned to dust now,

words would reconstruct me; I am mercury
escaped from a thermometer, each drop
scurrying to join another—pretty soon

I am risen like the phoenix, except next
time instead of foul breath, I will spit fire.
Who will firewalk my poems across such chasm?

for Jim, Denise, Charles, and Gaylord

Acknowledgments

Grateful acknowledgment is made to the editors and publishers for their support and permission to reprint the poems selected from the following previous collections:

Wings Press, San Antonio, Texas, for permission to reprint from *Garabato Poems* (1998); Tía Chucha Press, Chicago, Illinois, for permission to reprint from *You Come Singing* (1998); Bilingual Review Press, Tempe, Arizona, for permission to reprint from *In the Republic of Longing* (1999); University of Arizona Press, Tucson, Arizona, for permission to reprint from *Palm Crows* (2001); Louisiana State University Press, Baton Rouge, Louisiana, for permission to reprint from *Banyan* (2001); and University of Illinois Press, Urbana, Illinois, for permission to reprint from *Guide to the Blue Tongue* (2002).

Some of the new poems have appeared in the following journals and reviews, for which I thank their respective editors: *American Literary Review* ("Purple Finch"); *Antioch Review* ("The Exile Speaks"); *Bellevue Review* ("Tea Leaves, Caracoles,* Coffee Beans"); *Brilliant Corners* ("Poem for Eliades Ochoa, *Maestro del alambre dulce*"); *Kenyon Review* ("Japanese Magnolia"); *New England Review* ("La Florida"); and *Nimrod* ("Orange").

"La Florida" was chosen by Lyn Hejinian for *Best American Poetry* 2004, edited by David Lehman, published by Simon & Schuster, New York, 2004.

I would also like to express my deepest gratitude to my family, both in Cuba and the United States. To the Suarez-Poey family I will always be indebted for their love, support, and great food. I would like to thank my colleagues and staff at Bennington College for their friendship and generosity of spirit.

A heartfelt thanks and *abrazos* to Ed Ochester for having the *cojones* to allow me to do this collection while still in my early forties. His insights and editorial eagle eye made all the difference.

Virgil Suárez was born in Havana, Cuba, in 1962. Since 1974 he has lived in the United States. He is the author of four novels, *The Cutter*, *Latin Jazz*, *Havana Thursdays*, and *Going Under*, and of the story collections *Welcome to the Oasis* and *The Soviet Circus Visits Habana & Other Stories*. His memoirs, *Spared Angola: Memories of a Cuban-American Childhood* and *Infinite Refuge*, chronicle his life of exile in Cuba, Spain, and the United States. He is also the author of six previous collections of poetry: *Garabato Poems*, *You Come Singing*, *In the Republic of Longing*, *Palm Crows, Banyan*, and *Guide to the Blue Tongue*. As editor he has published the best-selling anthologies *Iguana Dreams: New Latino Fiction*, *Paper Dance: 55 Latino Poets*, *Little Habana Blues: Contemporary Cuban-American Writing*, *American Diaspora: Poetry of Displacement*, *Like Thunder: Poets Respond to Violence in America*, and *Vespers: Spirituality and Religion in America Poetry*. He is the recipient of fellowships from the NEA and the State of Florida Arts Council. He lives in Florida and loves the great city of Miami, where he spends time every chance he gets.